W9-CGX-361

HOW A SOLAR-POWERED HOME WORKS

Robyn Hardyman

Gareth Stevens
Publishing

Please visit our website, www.garethstevens.com. For a free color catalog of all our high-quality books, call toll free 1-800-542-2595 or fax 1-877-542-2596.

Library of Congress Cataloging-in-Publication Data

Hardyman, Robyn.
How a solar-powered home works / by Robyn Hardyman.
   p. cm. — (EcoWorks)
Includes index.
ISBN 978-1-4339-9549-1 (pbk.)
ISBN 978-1-4339-9550-7 (6-pack)
ISBN 978-1-4339-9548-4 (library binding)
1. Solar energy — Juvenile literature. 2. Solar houses—Juvenile literature. I. Hardyman, Robyn. II. Title.
TH7413.H37 2014
621.47—dc23

First Edition

Published in 2014 by
Gareth Stevens Publishing
111 East 14th Street, Suite 349
New York, NY 10003

© 2014 Gareth Stevens Publishing

Produced by Calcium, www.calciumcreative.co.uk
Designed by Simon Borrough and Paul Myerscough
Edited by Sarah Eason and Ruth Bennett

Photo credits: Cover: Shutterstock: Elena Elisseeva. Inside: Dreamstime: Airwolf01 24, Antoniosena 19, Erikreis 6, Monkeybusinessimages 5b, 8, Photosell247 20; Energy for Opportunity: 29t; Shutterstock: Anweber 1, 16, Mile Atanasov 9, Bennyartist 14, Rob Byron 13, M. Cornelius 11, Elena Elisseeva 15, Esbobeldijk 18, Paul Fleet 21t, Igor Kovalchuk 5t, lladyjane 7, Daleen Loest 26, Luiggi33 10, Joseph S.L. Tan Matt 21b, Neijia 2–3, NorGal 12, Ollirg 23, Joshua Resnick 22, YuriyZhuravov 4; Solar Roadways: 28–29; Wikipedia: CalderOliver 17t, Peellden 27, S-kei 17b, Solúcar 25.

Printed in the United States of America

CPSIA compliance information: Batch #CS13GS: For further information contact Gareth Stevens, New York, New York at 1-800-542-2595.

Contents

Energy from the Sun

The sun is a star: a huge burning ball of gases in space. It is so enormous, a million Earths would fit inside it. This flaming giant produces a massive amount of energy. Scientists have found ways to use some of this energy to meet our need for power.

Plants use the light of the sun to make food so they can grow.

Using the Sun

The sun lights our world and gives us heat. This light and heat make all life on Earth possible. Plants make food from sunlight, and animals eat plants. For thousands of years, people have been using the sun's light and heat. We have grown food crops in sunlight and concentrated the sun's rays to light fires. Now we are finding even better ways to harness this power.

Solar Power Up Close

Every minute, enough energy from the sun reaches Earth to meet the whole world's energy needs for a year. What's more, it takes that energy just 8 minutes to travel the 93 million miles (150 million km) to get here!

The sun is a massive generator of energy.

Why Do We Need Solar Power?

We use energy every day for hundreds of tasks, from switching on the lights to watching TV. Mostly this energy is in the form of electricity that is supplied by cables from a power station. Power stations can make electricity in different ways. Most of our electricity is made by burning huge quantities of coal, oil, and gas. These are called fossil fuels. They took millions of years to form underground. There is a limited amount of them, and we cannot make more. Coal, oil, and gas are not sustainable. Burning them also creates harmful pollution.

Our demand for energy is increasing all the time, as the population grows. We need to find cleaner, more sustainable sources of energy, such as the wind, the waves—and the sun.

We use electricity all the time at home, at school, and at work.

Using Solar Power

Solar power is created using the energy from the sun. This energy comes in two forms: heat and light. We can use both of these to meet our increasing need for energy in our homes. In the future, the way we design and build our homes will be affected by how we power them.

Passive Solar Power

Have you noticed how sunlight streaming through a window can make your home feel warmer, even on a cold day? That's passive solar heating in action. Our homes can be designed to make the best use of both the heat and the light of the sun. We can build our homes to get the most sunlight through the windows.

The sun lights and warms our homes during the day.

Smart Design

In the northern hemisphere, we need to build buildings that face south. We can also trap the heat of the sun in buildings by insulating them well. This means building walls and roofs with materials that stop the heat from escaping.

Cool in Summer

In summer, too much sunshine streaming in through large windows may make rooms overheat. Buildings can be designed with overhangs on the outside to shade large windows and keep everyone comfortable.

In a yard, we trap the heat of the sun in a greenhouse to help our food and flower plants grow.

Passive Solar Power Up Close

People in ancient times understood all about passive solar power. The ancient Greeks built whole cities of houses that were positioned to be warmed by the sun in winter, while blocking its heat in summer. The ancient Romans were the first to put glass in windows. They had learned that in winter this made rooms warmer as well as brighter.

Thermal Solar Power

Thermal solar power is created using the heat of the sun. Thermal solar power is used to heat water. In an average home, a person uses 15–25 gallons (70–114 l) of hot water every day for showers, baths, laundry, or washing dishes. Instead of using gas or electricity to heat the water, we can use the sun!

Using the sun to heat your water is a great way to save money and to also help the environment.

How It Works

A solar water heater heats up household water before it enters the home's conventional gas or electric water heater. The sun's heat is collected by a device on the roof of a building, called a collector. Flat plate collectors are the most common type. Collectors are installed on a south-facing slope or roof. They heat water that is then pumped to a storage tank.

When you turn on the faucet, heated water from the storage tank flows into the conventional water heater. If it is hot enough, it comes out as it is. If not, the gas or electric heater makes it hotter.

Where It Works

Solar water heaters heat only water when the sun is shining on them. This means that they are ideal for sunny places, where they can provide almost all of a household's hot water. They are less suitable for cloudy locations.

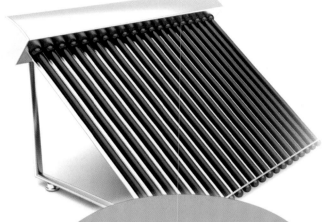

This evacuated tube collector is positioned to face south, to absorb the maximum amount of heat from the sun.

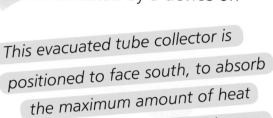

Heating Water

The most up-to-date type of collector is an evacuated tube collector. It heats water effectively. It consists of a series of metal pipes containing a liquid that heats up. Each pipe is enclosed in a double-walled glass tube, painted black to absorb heat. The air between the walls of the glass tube is removed (or evacuated), creating a vacuum. This works just like a vacuum flask, keeping in the heat.

Thermal Solar Power Outdoors

Thermal solar power can be used for many things aside from giving us hot showers at home. Outdoors, it can be used to heat swimming pools, so we can enjoy swimming all year round. Another use is even more vital—to cook food!

Hot and Sunny

Using the power of the sun to heat the water in an outdoor pool makes good sense. Outdoor pools are mostly located in warm, sunny places, where there is plenty of solar energy. Simple solar collectors are installed on a sloping roof near the pool, usually the roof of the pool house. They can easily heat the water of the typical pool to between of 75°F and 85°F (24°C and 30°C).

Solar collectors on the pool house roof heat the pool water to a comfortable temperature.

Cooking with the Sun

Solar cooking is a simple and safe way to cook food. It uses no electricity or fire. For the millions of people around the world who do not have access to electricity, solar cooking is an important breakthrough. Traditional cooking methods, which involve fires fueled by wood or dung, can be bad for the health and the environment. Solar ovens enable people to cook cleanly and for free. Solar ovens can also be used to boil drinking water to make it safe.

Solar ovens are an inventive way to use the sun's heat to power our lives.

ECO FACT

How a Solar Oven Works

A simple solar oven is a box surrounded by reflective panels. These direct the sunlight onto the food, which is placed inside a closed cooking pot. The food is cut into small pieces to help it cook quicker. The oven is put out in full sunshine, and cooking takes place over several hours. Although this is longer than with a fuel-based oven, the food can be left unattended. Food cooks fastest during the hottest part of the day.

Electricity from Sunlight

We've been using the heat of the sun for all of human history. But in the past 50 years there has been a big breakthrough—we have found out how to use the sun's energy to make electricity!

This calculator is powered by tiny photovoltaic panels.

Sun Power

Electricity powers almost everything we do. Making electricity directly from sunlight is efficient, because the energy supply will never run out. Also, solar power creates no pollution. Sunlight is turned into electricity using solar panels, in a process called photovoltaics, or PV. Small PV panels have been used to power devices such as calculators and clocks for decades. To make enough electricity to power our homes, we need bigger and better systems.

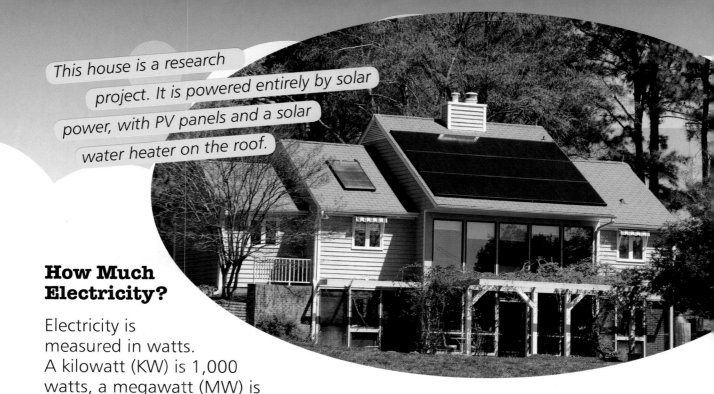

This house is a research project. It is powered entirely by solar power, with PV panels and a solar water heater on the roof.

How Much Electricity?

Electricity is measured in watts. A kilowatt (KW) is 1,000 watts, a megawatt (MW) is 1 million watts. We measure the electricity used over time in kilowatt hours or megawatt hours. The average American household uses 600 kilowatt hours of electricity per month.

An energy-efficient home uses less than that. People in the United States use more megawatt hours than anywhere else in the world. In a sunny climate, a 2 kilowatt PV system can produce 300 kilowatt hours of electricity per month.

ECO FACT

Discovering Solar Electricity

Solar electricity may be an energy solution of the future, but it was discovered by a French physicist, Edmund Bequerel, nearly two centuries ago. In 1839, he found that some materials generate very small amounts of electricity when they are exposed to sunlight. More than a century later, in 1954, Bell Laboratories developed a photovoltaic panel that consumers could use.

How Solar Cells Work

A photovoltaic solar panel is made up of a number of photovoltaic cells joined together. It is in each of these cells that the electricity is made.

A Solar Cell

Solar cells are made of several layers that are joined together. The top layer is glass, for protection. The next is a dark layer to keep the sunlight from reflecting off the glass. Under that are two thin wafers made of silicon and metal wires. The wafers are made by heating the silicon to a very high temperature. Chemicals are added to it that make particles in the silicon, called electrons, less tightly bonded to each other. When sunlight hits the silicon wafers, the electrons absorb some of the sun's energy. This makes them start to move, and they flow along the metal wires. This movement of electrons is an electric current, or electricity.

Some solar panels, such as these PV cells, are more efficient than others.

Photovoltaic Panels

Photovoltaic cells are joined together to make modules. These modules are then combined to make PV panels. The panels are installed on the roof of a building. The number of panels used depends on how much power is going to be needed in the building. The panels must be installed so that they get as much sunlight as possible. This means putting them on a south-facing roof, tilted up at an angle.

Too Hot?

Excessive heat is not good for solar panels—it makes them perform less well. A panel will produce more electricity on a sunny, cold day (especially if snow is reflecting the sunlight), than on a hot, clear day.

PV panels are installed on a south-facing roof, at an angle.

Solar Cells Up Close

The most efficient PV modules, the ones that convert more of the sun's energy into electricity, are modules with polka dots or octagons. They are usually very dark, or black. The less efficient ones are pure blue.

The Solar System

The solar panel creates electricity for your home, but how does it actually connect to your power supply? First, the electricity must be made safe for using in the home. It must also be stored, so that it can be used at times when the panels are not able to generate electricity.

Using Your Solar Power

The PV panels on the roof can be connected to a battery, which stores the electricity. This means that you can use the power at any time. Your house can also be connected to the grid, the main utility network. The grid will supply power if you have not generated enough from your solar panels. If you connect your PV system to the grid and don't have a battery, your PV will shut down in the case of a power outage.

This house has a large area of PV panels to provide its electricity.

Make Money from Solar

If your solar panels are generating more electricity than you need, you can give the excess back to the utility, and they pay you for it.

This process is called net metering. Your home electricity meter shows whether you are taking power from the grid or giving it back. If you give it back, the meter goes backward! Many states in the United States now allow net metering.

PV panels can be installed on apartment blocks, too.

Electricity Up Close

The electricity produced by PV panels is direct current (DC) but we need alternating current (AC) electricity to power our homes. In the solar power system, the electricity is converted from DC to AC in a device called an inverter. The electricity is then directed to the fuse box, where it is channeled to power different areas of the house, such as lights and sockets.

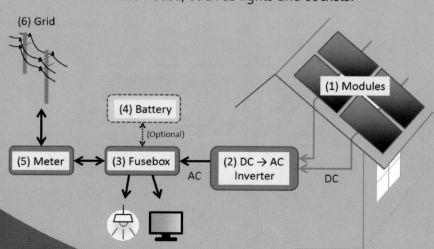

(6) Grid

(1) Modules

(4) Battery

(Optional)

(5) Meter ⟷ (3) Fusebox ← (2) DC → AC Inverter

AC   DC

A Regular Supply

You have set up your solar panels on the roof, and on a sunny day they make lots of electricity. But what happens when the sun isn't shining? It's vital to have a regular power supply you can rely on.

Sunshine or Cloud?

PV panels can only produce electricity when the sun is shining on them. They are most effective at midday, in full sun. When the sun is low in the sky, at the beginning and end of the day, or in winter, less sunlight falls on them and they are less effective. In a sunny place such as southern California or Texas, there are around 5.5 hours of "usable" sunshine available every day.

On a cloudy day these PV panels will make less electricity than in full sunshine.

PV Panels Up Close

The number of PV panels a home needs depends on how much power is used, and on the local climate. To generate 2 kilowatts of power you need around 240 square feet (22.3 square m) of solar panels, which is a big area. By reducing your electricity consumption, you will need fewer panels. This can be done by insulating the home, using energy-efficient appliances, and by turning things off!

On a flat roof, PV panels can be angled to get the most sunlight possible.

Storing Power

So how can your solar-powered home keep going when it is cloudy or during the night? In bright sunlight, the panels may have made more electricity than your home needs. This excess electricity is stored in the battery, ready for watching TV, washing dishes, or simply lighting the home at night.

Solar Electricity Outside

As well as providing electricity for appliances and lighting inside your home, the sun can power lots of outdoor devices.

Solar-powered lights can be an attractive, energy-efficient design feature in the garden.

Lights at Night

Solar-powered lights are great for places where it can be difficult to get electric cables. They are powered by the sun during the day, so they can shine at night! Large lights can be installed in the yard to give safety and security after dark. They can even be designed to come on automatically when they detect movement. Each light has its own PV panel to make electricity, which is stored in a small battery and used at night.

Tough LED

Many solar outdoor lights now use a new kind of fitting inside the bulb, called LED. This stands for "light-emitting diode." LED lights can withstand the rain and sun, and last for much longer than traditional bulbs. They also use much less energy, so your sunlight goes farther! LEDs are often found in garden lights. These are small decorative lights you simply stick in the ground. As with all solar-powered lights, they are not linked by wires, so there's no risk of accidents and they can easily be moved around.

This satellite is powered by hundreds of PV panels.

The Ultimate Outdoors

Solar panels are used somewhere else outdoors—way out in space! The satellites that travel around Earth to create our communication systems are covered in many PV panels. That is what powers them.

ECO FACT

This roadside sign is powered by PV cells.

Sending a Message

Next time you're on the highway, look out for the big flashing signs with messages for motorists. They are operated by solar power—you'll see they have solar panels above them, and a battery to store the electricity, so that they work 24 hours a day. Solar-powered signs can be found closer to home, too. You may see them at intersections or on the roadside. There are even solar-powered streetlights and parking meters.

The Limitations of Solar Power

Solar power has many advantages. We will never run out of power from the sun, and creating electricity from it does not produce any pollution—it is truly eco-friendly. It does have a few disadvantages, however. These are the reasons why solar power has not taken over from burning fossil fuels.

A PV cell can convert only up to 20 percent of the sun's light energy into electricity.

More Power Please

Solar panels can convert only around one-fifth of the energy in sunlight into electricity. The rest is wasted. This is not very efficient. Coal-fired power stations convert around one-third of the coal's energy into electricity. Scientists are working hard to improve solar power's efficiency, but it has limited the use of this new technology.

The Costs Up Close

A major factor affecting the popularity of solar power is the cost. Solar panels are expensive to make, and to install. For an individual, using a solar-power system will pay for itself in the long term by greatly reducing electricity bills and maintenance costs. Making electricity with solar power costs a lot more than burning coal and gas. But, if you factor in the cost of using up all our fossil fuels, and the damage to the environment through climate change, it doesn't seem so expensive.

Old Habits

They say "old habits die hard," and it's true that people often hesitate before they change something that is already working fine. Many people are resistant to changing the way they use energy.

Making the Change

We already have many coal-fired power stations and plenty of electricity from the grid, so why switch? Maybe it will be your generation that will lead the way in making solar power more affordable and widely used worldwide.

Solar power is expensive to install, but it saves users money in the long term as the sunlight is free.

Solar Power for Everyone

Solar power is not just for individual homes and businesses. It can be generated in solar power stations and distributed to everyone. Just like solar power options in your home, there are thermal and photovoltaic solar power stations, too.

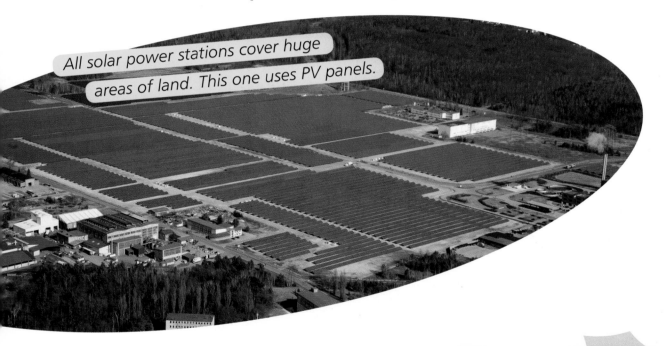

All solar power stations cover huge areas of land. This one uses PV panels.

Photovoltaic Power Stations

PV power stations use thousands of panels to create electricity, which is then connected to the grid.

The Agua Caliente plant in Arizona is the largest in the world. Another massive one, the Topaz Solar Farm, is under construction in San Luis Obispo County, California.

Thermal Power Stations

The world's first commercial thermal solar power station, called Solucar, opened in Spain in 2007. In the countryside, a massive tower is surrounded by a field of 600 huge mirrors. Each mirror reflects the sunlight and focuses it on one place at the top of the tower.

The tower at Solucar is 377 feet (115 m) tall, and the huge mirrors track the sun as it moves across the sky.

The intense heat created by the reflected light heats up water, which produces steam. This steam runs turbines, or huge engines, which generate power. As a result, enough electricity is produced to power up to 6,000 homes in the area.

Even Bigger

A much bigger solar power station will soon start operating in California in the Mojave desert. The Ivanpah Solar Electric Generating System includes 170,000 mirrors and three towers. It can produce around the same amount of electricity as one medium-sized fossil fuel power plant.

ECO FACT

First Solar Power Stations

The first thermal solar power stations have hundreds of curved mirrors. These concentrate the sun's rays to heat a special liquid that passes next to them in a pipe. The heat in this liquid then heats water and creates steam to run a turbine, as in the newer thermal system. The mirrors are called "parabolic troughs."

Where in the World?

Some countries have taken up solar power more than others—and the most solar-savvy countries aren't always the sunniest! Other factors affect the development of this eco-friendly energy, too.

Huge Growth

The solar industry is growing fast worldwide. The United States installed as much solar capacity in 2012 as it did in the entire last decade. New solar power plants will add a lot more capacity in future years. Germany and China now lead the world in the production of PV panels.

The Developing World

In countries where the supply of electricity is poor, solar power can make a huge difference. India has large power stations in development. In Africa, plans are introducing small solar systems to bring power to areas where there is no electricity grid.

In many African countries, solar power is bringing electricity to rural areas for the first time.

Making Solar Pay

One of the drawbacks of solar power is the high cost of getting started. In some countries, people have been given financial help to "go solar." Organizations contribute toward the start-up costs, or pay customers for any electricity they put back into the grid.

The government in Germany has pledged to get 25 percent of all its electricity from solar power by 2050. Germany tops the list of solar producers worldwide. California has also set ambitious targets for solar power. A new law requires utilities to get one-third of their electricity from renewable sources, including solar power, by the year 2021.

In Taiwan, this amazing new National Stadium opened in 2009. It has 8,844 PV panels on the roof!

Global Solar Power Up Close

This table shows the top 10 producers of PV solar power in 2011. If you add in thermal solar power production, Germany is top and the United States is second.

Producers of PV Solar Power in 2011

Country	Megawatts Produced
Germany	24,800
Italy	12,700
Japan	4,700
United States	4,200
Spain	4,200
China	2,900
France	2,800
Czech Republic	2,000
Belgium	1,800
Australia	1,200

Solar-Powered Future

Solar power's share of the world's energy output is small but growing fast. New technology is making PV panels more efficient. As they become more popular, the costs are really coming down, too. People are having new ideas for ways to use this great, eco-friendly technology.

New Technology

Since the beginning of 2010, the price of silicon PV panels has dropped by 30 percent, and costs are still falling. This makes it an even more attractive choice for homes and businesses. A new kind of PV panel, called thin-film PV, is even cheaper to make. It may be less efficient than silicon cells, but it's perfect for large-scale projects, such as PV power stations.

New Ideas

People everywhere are developing amazing ideas for using solar power. How about see-through solar panels to use as windows or porch railings? Or solar highways? Roads made of solar panels could charge your electric car as you drive! Heating elements in streets and sidewalks could melt ice and snow. These ideas are all being explored.

The future will bring many creative new uses for solar power, such as this solar-panel highway.

New Opportunities

Countries in the developing world need access to electricity to allow them to grow and improve the quality of people's lives. Solar power can make a huge difference. Building solar power plants in sunny locations can bring power to large areas. On a smaller scale, solar panels on individual buildings can bring power to villages for agricultural use or essential health services.

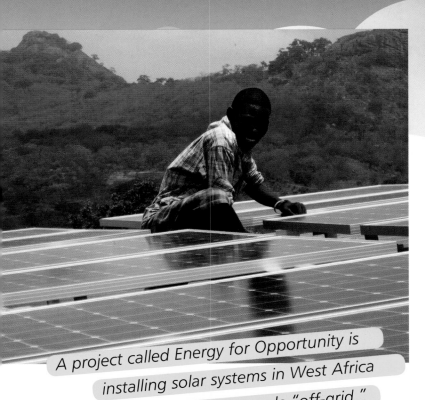

A project called Energy for Opportunity is installing solar systems in West Africa to bring electricity to people "off-grid."

ECO FACT

Solar Future

A new kind of thin-film PV cell is being developed. It is made from copper, zinc, and tin, which are cheaper than the indium and gallium used in existing thin-film cells. They are more efficient, too. These cells can simply be printed onto a surface, giving them even more possible uses.

Glossary

alternating current (AC) a type of electricity used to power homes and businesses

battery a device for collecting and storing electricity

collector the part of a thermal solar system that collects the heat in sunshine

direct current (DC) the type of electricity produced by a solar PV panel efficient in a solar panel, good at converting the energy in sunlight into electricity

electrons very small particles found in all matter

evacuated tube collector a solar energy collector that uses a series of vacuum tubes to absorb the sunlight

flat plate collector a solar energy collector that uses a network of tubes under a flat glass surface to absorb the sunlight

fossil fuels matter formed from remains of plants and animals that is used to produce energy, such as, coal, oil, and natural gas

fuse box the place in a home from where the electricity is wired to all rooms

grid the network that distributes electricity from power stations to consumers

hemisphere one half of Earth

insulating covering or protecting something to prevent heat being lost from it

inverter the device in a PV solar system that converts DC electricity to AC electricity for safe use

net metering when an electric meter can run backward if it is measuring electricity being sent back to the grid instead of being taken from it

passive solar heating when the heat of the sun naturally warms a building by shining on it or through windows

photovoltaics (PV) the process of creating electricity from the light of the sun

photovoltaic cell the smallest part of a solar power system, where the sunlight is converted to electricity

pollution the release of dirt or harmful substances into an environment

silicon a substance derived from sand that is used to make one kind of PV cell

sustainable having to do with a source that will never run out, such as the sun or wind

thermal solar power power created using the heat of the sun

thin-film PV a type of photovoltaic cell made using substances other than silicon

turbine an engine driven by a flow of steam

utility a company that produces and distributes electricity to consumers

vacuum a space with no air in it

watt the unit of measurement for electricity

For More Information

Books

Bearce, Stephanie. *Tell Your Parents: How to Harness Solar Power for Your Home*. Hockessin, DE: Mitchell Lane, 2009.

Friend, Robyn C. *A Clean Planet: The Solar Energy Story*. Marina del Rey, CA: Cascade Pass, 2010.

Hantula, Richard. *Energy Today: Solar Power*. New York, NY: Chelsea House, 2010.

Orme, Helen. *Earth in Danger: Energy for the Future*. New York, NY: Bearport, 2008.

Rooney, Anne. *Energy for the Future and Global Warming: Solar Power*. New York, NY: Gareth Stevens Publishing, 2007.

Websites

Find more useful information at Solar Energy International at:
www.solarenergy.org/answers-younger-kids

Visit the Energy Star website to learn more about energy-efficiency and saving money at:
www.energystar.gov

Be inspired by this website about the science behind climate change at:
www.acespace.org

Index